WE CAN SAVE THE EARTH

RECYCLE IT
ONCE IS NOT ENOUGH

Written by:
Stuart A. Kallen

Published by Abdo & Daughters, 6535 Cecilia Circle, Edina, Minnesota 55439

Library bound edition distributed by Rockbottom Books, Pentagon Tower, P.O. Box 36036, Minneapolis, Minnesota 55435

Library of Congress Number: 90-083599   ISBN: 1-56239-000-7

Cover Illustrated by: C.A. Nobens
Interiors by: Kristi Schaeppi

65760

Edited by: Jill Wheeler

TABLE OF CONTENTS

INTRODUCTION

The world is filling up with garbage! Aluminum (ah-loom-in-um) cans clutter the roadside. Bottles float in lakes and streams. And plastic is found just about everywhere. Every day we hear about litter and pollution. But what can we do about it?

Many of the numbers in this book are big numbers. Millions of cans, billions of tons. This shows what a huge problem we have on our hands. But every person either makes the problem worse or helps make things better. Those are our choices.

Making things better is easy. It just means choosing a glass bottle instead of a plastic one in the store, and then recycling the glass. Recycling can be fun and easy. After awhile, it becomes a habit to recycle. Soon, you don't even notice any effort.

If 250 people recycled just one can a day, we would save over 3,000 gallons of gasoline every year. Now, try 250,000 people recycling just one can a day. Then the savings would be **3 million gallons** of gas every year. If everybody recycled all the cans, the savings would be in the trillions. All of that means less air pollution and a better world for everyone. So you see, there are many things we can do about the garbage problem. The contribution of you and your friends is very important to our world. After all, this is the world that your children will live in, too.

What Is Recycling?

When we go to the store, we buy things in many different kinds of packages. Soft drinks, for example, come in bottles, aluminum cans and plastic containers. If we throw the container in the garbage when we're done using it, it goes to a garbage dump or landfill. There, wind, rain and sun slowly eat away the container. This process is called *biodegrading* (by'-oh-dee-grade-ing). The problem is that it takes 3,000 years for a glass bottle to biodegrade. Cans take 500 years. Plastic is not biodegradable and may be in a landfill forever.

Why Is That A Problem?

The average American family produces 100 pounds of trash a week! **Fourteen billion pounds** of trash are dumped into the ocean every year. In America, 500 new dumps are needed every year. Most people do not want new landfills in their neighborhoods because they pollute the water, attract animals and smell bad. Burning trash sends poisonous pollution into the air. Soon there will be nowhere to put all the garbage.

We can help solve the garbage problem if we recycle our bottles, cans, plastic and paper. When we recycle our trash, it is made into new things. Recycling helps eliminate the garbage problem and saves precious resources such as aluminum and trees. Here's a little information on where bottles, cans, plastic and paper come from, what they're used for and where they go when we recycle them. If everybody pitches in and recycles, our world will have less garbage and less pollution. The animals will be happier, and we'll be happier, too.

CHAPTER 1
Glass

The earliest glass made by humans was in Egypt around 5,000 years ago. For centuries, people have used glass for eating and drinking utensils, jewelry and artwork. Glassmaking is one of the oldest crafts in human history.

The main ingredient in glass is silica, a type of sand. Because silica melts at very high temperatures, it is mixed with lime (calcium oxide) and soda ash (sodium oxide) to lower its melting point. The three ingredients are mixed together and heated to more than 3,000 degrees Farhenheit. The elements selenium or manganese are mixed with the glass to color it.

After the glass is heated, the molten liquid is cooled to 2,000 degrees Fahrenheit. Then the glass is cut into gobs with large scissors. Next, measured amounts of glass are dropped into forming machines, where they are stamped into bottles. At modern bottle plants, computerized, automated machines produce about 140 containers a minute.

All the materials used in glass must be dug out of the earth. Many hillsides, forests and animals are destroyed during the mining process. Large amounts of oil are used to heat glass to 3,000 degrees Fahrenheit. Oil is a non-renewable resource, and burning it causes air pollution.

At recycling plants, glass is cleaned, crushed and remelted. It takes much less energy to recycle old bottles than it takes to make new ones. Using returnable bottles is the best option of all.

Returnable Bottles

When you buy returnable bottles, you leave a small amount of money for a deposit. When you bring the bottles back, your deposit is returned to you. Returnable bottles go back to the company that filled them, and they are sterilized and refilled. The same bottle is used over and over.

In the 1960's more than 60 percent of beverage containers in the U.S. were returnable. In the 1990's, only 12 percent are returnable. Throwaway bottles use three times more energy than returnable, reusable bottles.

Glass Facts

- 75 percent of the glass made in America is used for packaging.

- Each year we throw away 28 billion glass bottles and jars. That's enough to fill the tallest building in the world (the World Trade Center) 52 times.

- The energy saved from recycling one glass bottle will keep a light bulb burning for 4 hours.

- Recycling glass reduces related water pollution by 20 percent and air pollution by 50 percent.

Easy Ways You Can Help

- Keep a box in your house to save glass. When the box is full, take it to your local recycling center.

- Buy soft drinks in returnable bottles.

CHAPTER 2
Aluminum

Aluminum is a metal that is much lighter than steel but almost as strong. It is very resistant to rust. Everything from cans to frying pans to airplanes are made with aluminum. The earth's crust is 8 percent aluminum, making it the most plentiful metal in the world. Although aluminum is common, the only way to obtain large amounts of it is from *bauxite* (bawx-ite). Bauxite is a mineral. It is more scarce and more expensive to make into metal. One-quarter of the world's bauxite comes from Australia. Jamaica and Brazil also have large deposits.

After bauxite is mined, it is mixed with lime and soda ash, the same two ingredients that are used in glassmaking. That mix is put under pressure and exposed to chemicals that separate the aluminum. After a drying process, aluminum crystals are left. The crystals are then heated to 1,500 degrees Fahrenheit and poured into molds much like glassmakers use. The result is an aluminum can that is lightweight and chills easily.

Making aluminum cans causes a lot of pollution. One aluminum plant in Texas discharges 359 million pounds of pollution every year. In fact, aluminum plants are the biggest polluters in America.

Aluminum Facts

- Every 3 months, Americans throw away enough aluminum to rebuild all the commercial airplanes in the country.

- If you throw away an aluminum can, it wastes as much energy as if you filled that can half full of gasoline and poured it on the ground. That's a lot of gas if you realize that Americans use more than 66 billion cans a year.

- Americans recycled more than 42 billion cans in 1989.

- About 70 percent of all metal made in America is used just once and then thrown away.

- The energy saved from one recycled can will operate a television for 3 hours.

More Aluminum Facts

- Recycling aluminum cuts related air pollution by 95 percent.
- Making a can from recycled aluminum uses 90 percent less energy than making a can from scratch.
- Aluminum is the most recycled material, and companies save $2 million a day from using recycled aluminum.
- Aluminum foil, pie plates and food trays are also recyclable.

Easy Ways You Can Help

Because aluminum is worth so much, recycling companies pay about a penny a can to people who recycle. Some people have earned hundreds of dollars picking up cans by the side of the road and recycling them. Ask your parents to help you recycle.

CHAPTER 3
Paper

Human beings have been making paper for thousands of years.Until the 1800's, paper was made mostly from rags and cotton cloth. In 1860, a process was developed that used wood fiber in papermaking. By 1904, 60 percent of the paper made in America was made from wood pulp. By the 1930's, almost all paper was made from wood.

To make paper, trees are cut down. The wood is then turned into chips. The chips are mixed with water and chemicals to form a pulp. Pumps spray the pulp onto a large moving screen in a papermaking machine. The water in the pulp drains away, leaving an even mat of fibers. The mat moves through a series of rollers that squeeze out the water, press the fibers together and dry them. The result is paper.

Papermaking is a very polluting industry. One paper plant in North Carolina pumps 40 million gallons of highly polluted water into the Pidgeon River **every day**.

The trees used for paper also produce oxygen and help clean the air we breathe. Cutting down forests leaves animals homeless and adds to air pollution. Forests are needed for the survival of the earth.

Paper Facts

- 100 million trees are cut down every year to make the paper for "junk mail." One-half of junk mail is thrown away unopened and unread.

- 500,000 trees are cut down to supply Americans with their Sunday newspapers every week.

- Americans use 50 million tons of paper every year. That equals 850 million trees.

- Making paper from recycled material reduces related energy consumption by 50 percent and air pollution by 95 percent.

- Every ton of paper that is recycled saves 17 trees, 7,000 gallons of fresh water and enough energy to heat a home for 6 months.

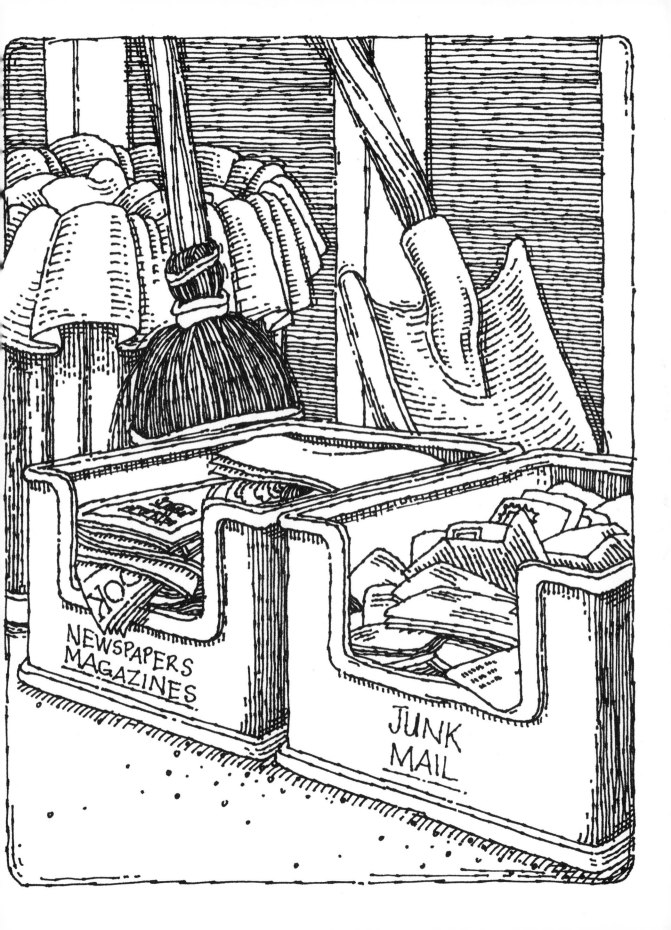

More Paper Facts

- It takes one 20-year-old tree to produce just 700 paper bags.
- Paper shopping bags are never made from recycled paper. Manufacturers say only new fiber makes a strong bag.
- More than one billion trees are used to make disposable diapers every year.

Easy Ways You Can Help

Keep a box in your house to save newspapers, junk mail, magazines and boxes. Then recycle them. Some recyclers pay for newspaper —check in your phone book for recyclers. If every American recycled just one newspaper a week, it would save 30 million trees every year.

Ask your parents to use cloth bags at the grocery store or when you go to the store take paper bags with you and reuse them.

CHAPTER 4
Plastic

Plastic is everywhere. There are many types of plastics used in everything from candy wrappers to rocket ships. Plastic is light and easily molded and does not rust or rot. The main types of plastics we will talk about here are the kinds used for wrapping food such as *Styrofoam* (sty-ro-foam) and *polystyrene* (poly-sty-reen).

Plastic is made from oil, coal or gas. Because oil is the cheapest of these materials, most plastic is made from oil. After the oil is pumped out of the ground, it is sent to a refinery where it is separated into different chemicals. Many of the chemicals are used as fuel, but some, especially *naphtha* (naf-the), are used to make plastic.

Once the naphtha is separated from the oil, it is processed again. A gas called *polyethylene* (poly-eth-il-een) is separated from the naphtha and turned into plastic. The plastic is then heated, dyed and poured into molds. Plastic can be almost as hard as metal or as flexible as a plastic bag. It can be used in paints, foam and fibers.

Almost everything about plastic causes pollution. When oil is pumped out of the earth, it pollutes the water and land around it. Oil spills like that from the Exxon tanker *Valdez* in 1989 polluted hundreds of miles of the beautiful Alaskan coastline with black, deadly goo. Whenever animals come in contact with oil, they become sick and often die.

After oil is turned into plastic, it does not biodegrade. A plastic bottle holding soft drinks still will be here 1,000 years from now. The gases that are used to make styrofoam, chlorofluorocarbons (cloro-floro-carbons), or CFC's, cause holes in the protective ozone layer that surrounds the planet. Every chemical used to make styrofoam causes cancer in humans. When plastic is burned, it gives off toxic gases that cause cancer.

Plastic Facts

- During a cleanup of a Texas beach, 15,000 plastic six-pack rings were found in 3 hours. These rings, which are used for canned drinks, are invisible to birds and fish. Birds looking for fish dive into the rings and become tangled. Young seals and sea lions get six-pack rings caught around their necks. As they get bigger, the rings slowly choke them to death.

More Plastic Facts

- Every year, America produces an amount equal to 10 pounds of plastic for every person on earth.

- Plastic bags and Styrofoam are swallowed by whales, fish, turtles and birds. The plastics cause the animals to die.

- Every year, Americans produce enough Styrofoam cups to circle the earth 436 times.

- Americans use 2.5 million plastic bottles **every hour**!

- The ink used to print on plastic bags contains a deadly poison that is released into the air when burned.

- The world's shipping industry dumps 450,000 plastic containers into the ocean **every day**!

- If one out of ten Americans bought products with less plastic packaging every month, it would eliminate 144 million pounds of plastic from our dumps and reduce air pollution.

Easy Ways You Can Help

Before you toss six-pack rings in the garbage, snip each circle with a scissors.

Pick up plastic litter and six-pack rings when you're out walking.

It's easy to wash out plastic bags and reuse them.

There is no such thing as good Styrofoam or polystryene. Don't use it. Try not to buy any products that come packaged in Styrofoam. If you eat in fast food restaurants, ask for paper plates and cups.

Don't purchase soft drinks or food in plastic bottles.

If you must use bags at the store, use paper bags.

Find out if you can recycle plastic in your town, if so, separate your garbage from your plastics and set it outside to be picked up by the collectors.

CHAPTER 5

Batteries

Batteries are amazing things. We put them in our flashlight and toys, and they give us power anywhere. But batteries contain deadly poisons such as mercury. When batteries are thrown out, they go to garbage dumps, where they corrode. Then, the poisons in the battery run into rivers, lakes and streams when it rains. If batteries are burned with garbage, they release poisons into the air.

Battery Facts

- Americans use 2 billion disposable batteries every year.

- 40 percent of all batteries are bought during the Christmas holidays.

- 50 percent of the mercury used in America is used in batteries.

Easy Ways You Can Help

Buy rechargeable batteries. They cost more at first but last for a very long time. When you have rechargeable batteries and a recharger, you never have to worry about dead batteries. Just charge 'em up. Ask your parents for a battery recharger and rechargeable batteries.

Recycle your batteries.

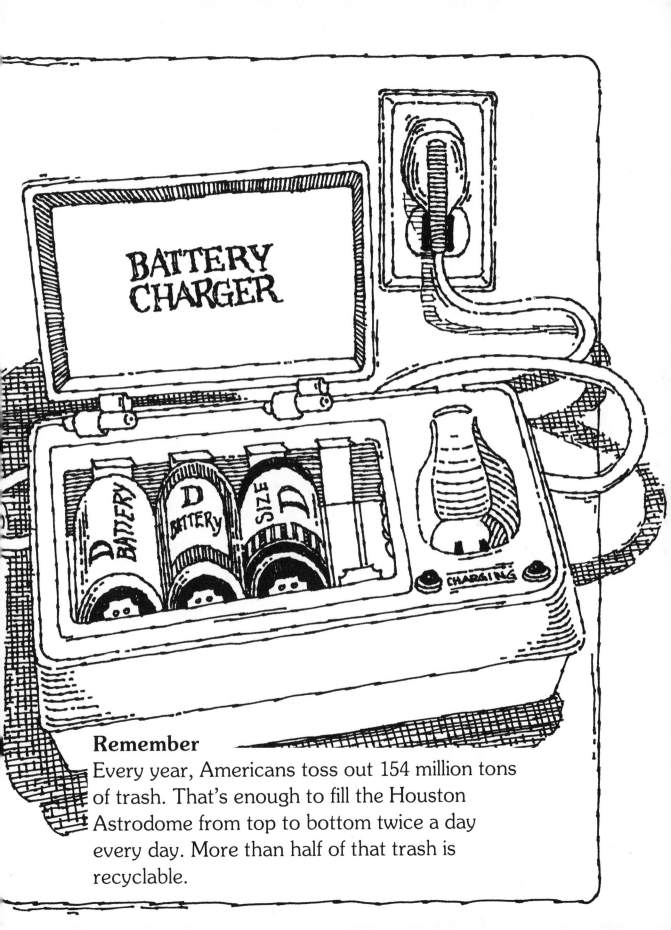

Remember
Every year, Americans toss out 154 million tons of trash. That's enough to fill the Houston Astrodome from top to bottom twice a day every day. More than half of that trash is recyclable.

WHAT ELSE CAN YOU DO?

If you want to write or call local officials, you can make a difference. Politicians and large companies want to hear from kids and young adults. Find out the names of your state and national representatives in the phone book or library.

You can also organize class picnics to parks or beaches to clean up litter. Share the information in this book with your parents and friends, and get them involved in cleanup efforts.

If you do not have one, start a recycling program in your community. Have your class contact your city's mayor and ask about recycling.

Plant trees to improve air quality. Walk or ride a bike instead of driving. And, above all, recycle!

WHO TO WRITE TO — WHO TO CALL

TO STOP JUNK MAIL — Write to Mail Preference Services, Direct Marketing Association, 11 West 42nd St., P.O. Box 3861, New York, N.Y. 10163. They'll stop your name and your parents name from being sold to mailing companies. This should reduce about three-quarters of the junk mail you and your parents receive.

TO RECYCLE PAPER — Write the Paper Recycling Committee, American Paper Institute, 260 Madison Ave., New York, N.Y. 10016, or call (212) 340-0600 for pamphlets on paper recycling.

TO RECYCLE GLASS — Write Glass Packaging Institute, 1801 K St. N.W., Washington, D.C. 20006 or call (202) 887-4850 for free pamphlets on glass recycling.

TO RECYCLE ALUMINUM — Write The Aluminum Association, 900 19 St. N.W., Washington, D.C. 20006. You can receive free information on aluminum recycling.

FOR LOCAL RECYCLING INFORMATION —Call the Environmental Defense Fund's toll free hotline; 1-800-CALL-EDF. They'll answer all your recycling questions. It's free!

TO STAMP OUT STYROFOAM — Write The Ecology Center, 2530 San Pablo Ave., Berkely, CA 94702. Send a self-addressed, stamped envelope for free information about eliminating harmful Styrofoam.

A FINAL WORD

The information in this book is just a start toward cleaning up the environment. People who are in school now will be needed in the future as scientists, engineers, writers, artists and researchers in environmental research. Many jobs that don't even exist today will grow around our need to clean up our world. Now that you're interested in recycling - DO IT! And find other ways to help the world as well. The world needs your help, and we owe it to ourselves and our children to keep working. We need you.

GLOSSARY

ALUMINUM: A light, soft, silvery-white metal. Aluminum is the most common metal found in the earth.

BAUXITE: The main mineral of aluminum.

BIODEGRADABLE: Capable of being broken down by wind, rain, sun or by other natural processes.

CHLOROFLUOROCARBONS (CFCs):: A group of compounds that contain the elements carbon, chlorine, fluorine and sometimes hydrogen and are used to make plastics and other solutions.

CORRODE: To eat or wear away, little by little.

DISPOSABLE: Something that is designed to be used once and then thrown away.

LANDFILL: An area built up by burying layers of trash between layers of dirt.

MERCURY: A heavy silver-colored metal.

NATURAL RESOURCE: A material found in nature that is useful or necessary for people to live.

OZONE LAYER: The upper layer of the earth's atmosphere containing ozone gas that blocks out the sun's harmful ultraviolet rays.

PLASTIC: A man-made material that can be molded and shaped when heated.

POLLUTION: Harming the environment by putting man-made wastes in the air, water and ground.

POLYSTYRENE: A rigid, see-through plastic.

PULP: A soft, wet mass of material. Chemicals and water are added to wood chips to make wood pulp.

RECHARGE: To restore the active materials in a battery.

RECYCLE: Reusing materials instead of wasting them.

REFINERY: A place where crude oil and other substances are made pure.

STERILIZE: To free from dirt and germs.

STYROFOAM: A flexible form of plastic used for packaging.

TRASH: Worthless objects that are thrown away.

INDEX